MYLES OF LIFE WITHIN ME

The Journey of
Losing a Child

Published by Phyllis Owens
Printed in the United States of America 2013—First Edition
Second Edition Printed 2024
Cover Design by Ana Saunders of Es3lla Designs

Library of Congress Cataloging-in-Publications Data
Myles of Life Within Me: The Journey of Losing A Child/Phyllis Owens

ISBN 979-8-218-39114-0 (pbk.) Second Edition

1. Owens, Phyllis 2. Loss 3. Loss of Child 4. Grief
5. Mourning 6. Personal Growth

Table of Contents

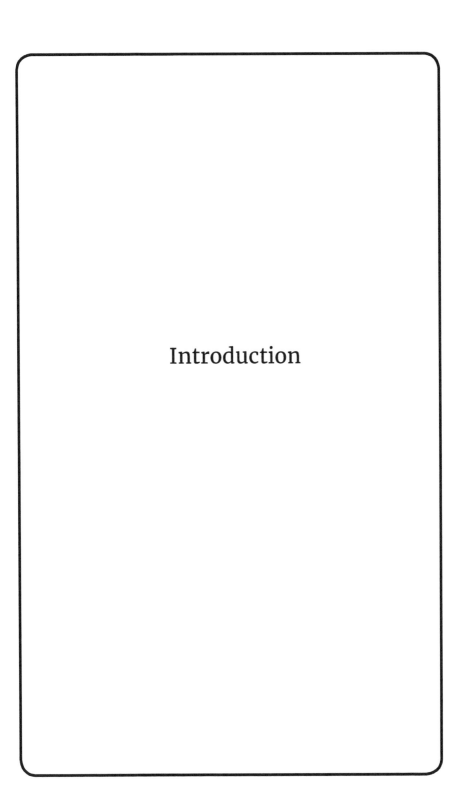

Introduction

*L*ife wasn't always a cloudy day. The sun *did* come out tomorrow. But tomorrow hasn't been in my neighborhood for quite some time.

I met the love of my life in computer school. He was an instructor at the school, and we connected immediately. The next thing I knew, we were driving to my cousin's wedding on a beautiful autumn day. I had no clue I would leave the reception as his fiancée.

It was an amazing proposal with a ring hidden in a glass of champagne. Lugene got on one knee and whispered those four unforgettable words: "Will you marry me?" I said yes. We started planning, and not before long, we were packing our bags in New York City, and moving to the suburbs of New Jersey to begin a wonderful life.

Soon after, my first child Quiana was born. I gave birth to a three pound-seven-ounce beauty! Her premature birth required Quiana to stay in the hospital for five weeks, but that was fine with me. I was just glad she had made it out alive. I visited her every day as I recovered from my cesarean section. I had an emergency cesarean section because I developed toxemia at seven months. So, the doctors were concerned about her lungs developing enough to deliver, but my blood pressure added to the drama. It was too high to continue the pregnancy. Feeding her two cc's of formula was joyous because she was eating, however looking at her while they shaved her hair in order to find an additional vein in her little body was painful. Thankfully, she survived it, and my baby girl came home in a little over a month's time.

My second child was a boy, 10 pounds 8 ounces; he was huge and active. It was another cesarean section but for different reasons. I was already one week late, and he was not in position yet to be born. I was miserable! I had gained 60 pounds and couldn't find anything around the house to wear—not a shoe, not a raincoat, nothing! Everything was much different with this birth, and when Myles was born, we were amazed by how big he was! He wore 6–9-month sized clothes at birth, and because his arms and legs were still short, we would just roll up the sleeves. He had big eyes like mine, and a beautiful smile.

My third pregnancy was another girl. Courtney rushed into the world weighing in at 7 pounds 6 ounces. Since I had never experienced a vaginal delivery, I decided to have an epidural so I could remain awake to see her birth. It was great to see her immediately and not to deal with pain, at least not until the medication subsided.

Life was going great, and all was going well. My daily routine included taking my 7-year-old daughter and 3-year-old son to summer camp and caring for my 3-month-old daughter. But on August 21, 1990, my normal life changed in a matter of minutes.

The phone rang.

The camp supervisor sounded startled. All I could make out was that my son was being rushed to the hospital. He was having convulsions. So I quickly called my husband and got dressed. The hospital was 5 miles away from my home and it took me 10 minutes to get there. I hurried into the emergency room. Myles had not yet arrived. Thoughts of sadness began to rush into my heart. Like a clogged faucet, I couldn't process my emotions. *What had happened? Why didn't they call me earlier? What is taking the ambulance so long to get here? It can't be major. Maybe Myles had a seizure. But seizures don't run in my family.* In all of five minutes, I thought about every conclusion possible, but no narration created in my mind could prepare me for what happened next.

I ran back outside. The ambulance was just arriving. I watched them roll my son into the hospital and I lost it. Everything seemed to happen in slow motion. My heart erupted into fury and confusion. A nurse grabbed my 3-month-old daughter from me, and my husband arrived just in time for us to be called into that cold, little room...the same room where they would tell us that my baby boy, Myles, had died.

CHAPTER ONE

It was a normal day...

The craziest thing about that day was how normal it was before I got the call. The morning was sunny and beautiful. The house was peaceful and quiet. After getting up, I walked into the kids' room to wake them, and we did our regular morning routine. I led them to the bathroom, helped them to get dressed and then we went downstairs to have breakfast.

The three of them slept together in the same room. The room was big enough to hold a twin bed with a trundle underneath and Courtney's crib. After changing Courtney's diaper on the changing table, I took her downstairs with me to warm her bottle. She could only drink Carnation milk because she was allergic to every other type, so I fed her, and then I fed Myles and Quiana and headed to summer camp.

No mother ever thinks, when dressing their child, this may be the last outfit he wears. No parent ever thinks, on a sunny summer day, let me kiss my baby twice just in case I don't see him again. Myles was wearing blue jeans, a white t-shirt and his Air Jordan sneakers. The summer camp was only fifteen minutes away from our house. It was a nice, tree-filled suburban neighborhood. As we approached the horse-shoe entrance to the red schoolhouse, I could see parents dropping off their children and the camp counselors waiting to receive them. As I pulled up, I got out to give them a hug and kiss. The last thing I said to Myles as I squatted down beside him was, "I love you. Have fun." He hugged me back replying, "I love you, too!"

What a beautiful sound to hear your child say those words. Parents, don't take these precious moments for granted.

We let go of our embrace and I stood there watching him walk away. He got into line with all the other kids and eagerly awaited his day to start. This was my cue to leave, so I proceeded to walk back to the car. I got in and drove away with Courtney in the back seat.

My day continued as normal. I stopped at the grocery store to pick up a few missing items from home, I put a load of laundry in the wash, and did a few other random things until about 1:00 p.m. Around 1 is when I received the phone call. I remember exactly where I was in the kitchen. As I fed Courtney who was perfectly placed in her highchair, I reached up to grab the phone on the wall behind her.

The director told me that Myles had been throwing up after having an object in his mouth. I later found out more details. It was naptime and Myles was lying down on his mat to take a nap with the other children. He noticed a green thumbtack on the floor and put it in his mouth. The thumbtack was used to hold a curtain up to the window, but it had fallen on the floor. The thumbtack got stuck in his throat. The doctors tried a tracheotomy to remove the tack, but it was impossible to revive him. Seconds after I got off the phone with the director, I called Lugene to let him know what was happening. Like the multi-tasking mom that I am, I prepared the quickest bottle ever and jetted out the door while grabbing some diapers for Courtney. I ran out of the house, placed her in the backseat, got into the car, backed out of my driveway and was on my way to the hospital.

The panic and shock and trauma that a mother feels is beyond words. In seconds, your entire life stops and ceases to exist. You hear the words "He did not survive," but you don't even process them. You scream because your body reacts to the sound of unbearable news, but your brain is on pause. It doesn't calculate. It doesn't make sense; and the first thing you think is, I must be dreaming. This has to be a terrible, horrible, unbelievable dream. You look around for made-up memories, for someone whom you do not know, for the music to start playing in the background. Surely this is a movie and I am just a play-play character—but then, the doctors turn around and walk out of that cold room. You realize, *this is real life.* My life will forever be changed. My baby boy, my pretty baby boy, who was so full of life and energy, is no longer going to say those three precious words, "I love you" again.

CHAPTER TWO

This can't be happening...

When I got to that hospital---the same hospital where I had given birth to Myles--- I ran inside to ask the reception desk if Myles Johnson was there. They looked at me like they didn't know what I was talking about. That's when I realized he had not arrived yet. I went back outside to wait for him there. I thought to myself, "Is this the right hospital?" I went back inside to double check with the front desk if they were absolutely sure they hadn't heard anything about my son. They again affirmed their previous answer, and I had no choice but to go outside again and wait. This time I heard it – the ambulance sirens in the distance.

Just imagine hearing that sound weeks later; months later; years later. Every time I hear an ambulance, it reminds me of this moment. Those who have never been through it may never understand the subtle and unexpected triggers that happen all the time, at all the wrong times. It was the sound of both possibility and disaster. The quicker they got him into the hospital, the better. All I could do was close my eyes and hope for the best.

As soon as the ambulance pulled in, its doors opened and out came EMTs with dark blue uniforms taking out Myles on a stretcher. He had on an oxygen mask and his shirt had been ripped off. Immediately I began to cry. Despite the fact I was telling them I was his mom, they rolled him right past me and left me no choice but to run behind them until we got to the operating room entrance. Beyond that point, I was not allowed.

Can you imagine being told "Do not enter" when on the other side of those doors, lies a baby who came from your womb? It was too difficult to believe, but rationally, I knew that doctors had to focus on the patient. Rationally, I understood that my presence in the room would only make things worse. But in moments like these, the last thing you want to be...is rational. Soon after, Lugene dashed in, went to me and then went to the nurses trying to find out more information regarding Myles' status. Nothing new was shared but finally a man in scrubs came out to escort us to a small room with a table in it. He not only informed us that they had to do a tracheotomy on Myles but also that he hadn't made it. I started screaming, "No!" and flipped the table over. We were asked if we wanted to see him and of course, we said yes.

We were escorted to where he was. His jeans and sneakers were still on and he was still warm to the touch. Lugene leaned over toward Myles and began to cry. It was happening to me, it was happening to us, but it felt like it was happening outside of us. I mean, I know my son had died, but I literally felt, at that moment, that I had died, too. We were allowed to stay with Myles for as long as we wanted to. They never rushed us. They didn't check in until we welcomed them in. I just sat there in silent agony—my body responded physically to the emotional pain my heart was feeling. I couldn't think of anything else except that my baby boy was no longer here to laugh, eat, and dance. I couldn't hear anyone around me. If they spoke, I am sure I didn't respond. Shock was an understatement. I was slammed into an anesthetic trance and didn't want to come out.

It was finally time to go home but I didn't want to go. I called my sister who came to join us at the hospital. The nurse gave Courtney to her, and after another hour, we went home. We came to the hospital in separate cars, so I went home with Lugene and left my car in the emergency room to be picked up the next day. Quiana was still at camp during all of this; so, we arranged for her to be picked up by my brother-in-law, Tyrone.

When Quiana saw that mommy wasn't picking her up, she knew something was wrong. All the way home, she kept asking about Myles because every day, they would wait in the same spot together. This time, Myles didn't come to the spot, and mommy didn't come pick her up. Like every child, Quiana knew this wasn't right. She kept asking Tyrone what had happened, but he didn't tell her the truth. He felt it wasn't his place to tell her. He simply told her Myles was sick and that's why he hadn't come home with her. When they arrived at our house, Lugene was on the couch, and I was upstairs in my bed. I was crying and, in a daze, and Quiana walked in and asked, "Where's Myles?" It was Lugene, her father, who finally told her the truth.

CHAPTER THREE

Dancing with a limp...

"You will lose someone you can't live without, and your heart will be badly broken, and the bad news is that you never completely get over the loss of your beloved. But this is also the good news. They live forever in your broken heart that doesn't seal back up. And you come through. It's like having a broken leg that never heals perfectly—that still hurts when the weather gets cold, but you learn to dance with the limp."
— Anne Lamott

If Anne Lamott's words are true, I've been limping for over twenty years. This new dance I have is so easy to do, I can't remember a time I wasn't dancing with a limp. The loss and pain I felt when it happened was incomparable to the moment when it all started sinking in. Just think about the first time you went to dial the number of the parent or spouse you lost. In my case, it was even more obvious because every room in the house had memories of Myles. His clothes, his chair, his toys, his scent. I could see him in everything. I could feel his presence, and sometimes catch myself laughing myself into violent tears. The memory of him overwhelmed me so much that I couldn't escape my own thoughts. It was terrorism of the mind. The one thing I loved more than anything in the world, was the opportunity to be a good mother. I love my babies! I love being able to take care of them and provide for them. But now, this was a permanent marker on a dry erase board. Every time someone came to see my life, they would see this permanent pain, and I didn't know what to do with it. At times, I held onto the pain like a warm blanket. It helped me feel Myles in the now. But at other times, I knew I was much too sad to be of help to anyone. It made me sadder to realize that I was sad. I didn't want to cry, but guess what I did? I cried.

I've got to say, there are a lot of things I do not remember. Many who mourn will grieve in different ways. Some will overcompensate and try to pretend it didn't happen. Others will stay stuck in the past and not move forward. For me, I was somewhere in the middle. I had two young girls, and I couldn't let them grow up without a mother. I had to take care of them, and I had to take care of the responsibilities in my home. But I don't remember much color in my life after Myles passed. Everything moved from red, orange and blue, to black, white and gray. I don't remember what it felt like not to have that cloud of sorrow hanging over every conversation; every outing; every vacation. I do remember my husband asking my doctor for a mild sedative for me because I was so emotional. I do not remember who arranged the funeral, I do not remember who came and who did not come. I do remember Myles' teacher coming by the house to offer condolences, but I was too hurt to hear anything. My husband and my brother-in-law, Tyrone, drove to three funeral homes before making the final decision. These men, along with my oldest brother and dad, were the rocks that stabilized me during this rough time. Together they arranged everything for the funeral. I remember my mother-in-law wanting to help by pressing my son's suit and white shirt, but I wanted to do it. I was adamant about taking care of my baby, so my husband said, "Let her do it." I don't remember making many phone calls. People just started showing up. But I do remember calling a friend at work to find out if I had life insurance for him; I did.

CHAPTER FOUR

The Wake...

I wonder why they call it a wake? When people pass away, why do they call that first hour of visitation a wake? I wish I could wake Myles up and go home. I wanted to wake him, grab him, and take him to the park, but it just couldn't happen. On August 24, 1990, it all started to settle in my mind. My youngest brother became so emotional during the program, the funeral director asked us to come to his office. He wanted to distract us from the emotional episode going on in the main room. The next day, we did the funeral and the burial. I did not know what I was going to wear because I had just had a baby 3 months ago. I had not lost the weight yet, and I did not really care much about impressing anyone. I just wanted my baby back.

But I found a long-sleeved black dress and I got dressed very slowly. I think the slower it took me to get dressed, the longer I could delay the moment. Funerals are the exact opposite of weddings. Brides are happy to get married but fashionably late. The attendees are excited about a new path of wonderful memories shared between two lovebirds, and the room is filled with anticipation, excitement and joy. Funerals are completely different. The family who is mourning is not really there. We show up because we have to; not because we want to. The day seems to drag along like a dismal rainy day. The words people say are genuine and beautiful, but we aren't really hearing them. We are polite but we just wish people would leave us alone. It's an occasion of deep sadness. Add to that the innocence of the 3-year-old baby, and the unexpected nature of the entire situation. My experience was an overnight stock market crash. Within minutes, our world was upside down---we weren't going on vacation. Instead, we were planning and heading to a funeral.

CHAPTER FIVE

Your words matter...

I wish people were more thoughtful about their words at funerals. You may not realize it, but your words, during a tender moment, can make or break a person. Take for example the expression "I know how you feel." Have you ever lost a loved one and someone said to you, "I know how you feel?" How did you respond? Did those words comfort you? Most people who are grieving don't want to hear this expression. Telling someone "I know how you feel" removes the personal experience that I had with my child. You didn't have the same memories. You don't share the same experiences. You don't know the level of relationship I had with my loved one. So, in my opinion, it would be better to say nothing at all than to say the wrong thing and shatter me forever.

At the burial, the priest said the wrong thing. It made me so angry I didn't want to see or hear anything else after that. It was a small comment, but it tore me to the core. He stood over the casket and pronounced, "God will take care of him." And immediately, I yelled out, "I TOOK CARE OF HIM!" I forgot where I was, I forgot who was around me—at that moment, I snapped. I now know that his intention wasn't to offend me, but my heart was so broken, and his words sounded as if he was implying that I hadn't taken care of my baby. It was almost like hearing, "Since you didn't do it, Phyllis, God had to take care of him. But don't worry, God has him." And that was not the truth! I loved Myles with an everlasting love. I loved all my children deeply, but Myles was a unique child. Everything he did was big. It was so filled with layers of love that I often found myself feeling like the greatest mother in the world. I was so fortunate to have these three little angels, and now, a priest was suggesting that I didn't take care of him.

Of course that isn't what he said, but the lesson here is to remember: your words matter. It's not always what you say, but it may be the way you say it. When someone is grieving, be sensitive and thoughtful. Say less and love more. Try not to run to "God language" because none of us know what God's will is completely. The more people tried to tell me that "God knew what He was doing," or "God had a better plan," the more I began to hate God. It didn't make sense to me that a loving God would look down from heaven, see my heart and take it away from me. It didn't make sense that I could be robbed of my baby from a freak accident that didn't even happen in my home. None of it made sense, so the "God" answers were not helping me.

They only made matters worse.

After the burial, my cousin escorted me to the limousine. The ride back was in full color, but my heart was on mute. I saw loved ones consoling loved ones. I saw trees and houses and other cars. I saw a train of benevolent cards stacked high on the seat. But I didn't see Myles. I didn't see my baby. The limo was driving away from the place they buried him, and I wasn't going to see him again. It was the worst kind of anesthesia a person could feel, because even though my heart felt numb, I was still awake to experience the pain.

When I got back to my house, I went upstairs and climbed in the bed.

CHAPTER SIX

Life on empty...

The morning after was full of emptiness. If emptiness were a color, it would look like dark gray water. It would sound like tedious dripping from an unfixed faucet. If emptiness were a cancer, mine was on stage 4. My heart was so empty that no tears could properly fill it. No words could really convey it. My mind was full of clashing cymbals, but my logic fell short of comprehension. I was in a bubble that seemed to pop every time I opened my eyes, and there I was today, realizing...empty is here again.

Empty noise from the kids' room. Empty hearts with a gaping, obvious hole in it. Empty house, without people. At this point, everyone had gone home. Empty conversations over breakfast. We spoke but we didn't communicate. After Myles died, none of our conversations moved past the surface. We reported to each other what was needed from the grocery store. We listed our daily tasks and bills. It was an empty refrigerator in my heart, and my soul was freezing to death. So, did I eat that day? I don't even know. I doubt I ate breakfast, lunch or dinner, but if I did, I know we didn't say much. Silence was the default to tears. Silence became the secret plague that kept us functional when we weren't emotional.

My eyes lids cracked open and the realization that I was still alive, with a limp, overwhelmed me.

What do I do now?

Should I go for a walk? No, because then I will see the neighbors taking their kids to church. Should I clean the house? No, because then I will have to bump into one of Myles' toys. Not ready for that. Should I bury myself under the covers and go back to sleep? No, because then I would have another horrible nightmare where I can see my baby suffering on that thumbtack and trying to catch his breath. No! All of it was just too much to think about. I needed a healthy distraction, but everyone had gone home; the house was...well, empty.

I remember sitting at the dining room table; I think my mother and mother-in-law were there with me, too. As tears fell from my eyes, I began reading the cards of condolences we had received. Words mean everything when you are speechless and full of sorrow. I read the cards, but I zeroed in on the comments written in blue or black ink. It was something so intimate and beautiful about my friends and family signing their name. My sister took 2 weeks off from work to help us care for our daughters. My mother and mother-in-law did the same. So, their presence was helpful.

When you don't know what to do, be present. When you don't know what to say, be present. When I was terribly overwhelmed by it all, their presence spoke volumes to me. I'm sure I didn't ask for them to stay, but that's what makes family so beautiful.

Family should do the right thing even if the grieving parent can't mouth the words. My family made sure that my girls were okay. They helped around the house. They were the dream team of grief. And as thankful as I was that they were with me, I kept wishing Myles would just come back. I cried every single day for at least a year or more. I cried until I had black rings around my eyes. I cried until my lungs lost energy. When I wasn't crying, I was plotting Myles' return. I wasn't ready to face the reality, so I thought about ways to bring him back. There had to be some method that had not yet been tried. Something the doctors could've done to make it all go away. Maybe in a moment, I would really wake up from what now felt like a three-week dream, and we would go back to normal. But no, it didn't happen that way. I wasn't dreaming. I didn't need to wake up. I was fully awake, and fully without.

CHAPTER SEVEN

Trying to move on...

I kept making it harder for myself, or if it was really moving on was harder than I thought. I don't know if this was hard. But I know I couldn't do it! I just couldn't do it.

A few weeks later, school began for my 7-year-old daughter. Every morning I had to get her ready, prepare breakfast, feed my 3-month old daughter and drive her to school. Quiana later tells me that it was a sad day for her every time she looked to the right side of the car and did not see Myles. The routine pattern was so engrained in her that the opposite reality overwhelmed her. Imagine every morning waking up to go to school and knowing that all your teachers know what you still don't want to accept. It was so difficult for us. She cried sometimes, and I cried all the time. Just seeing children go to school, run in the park, leap in their parents' arms, made me wish my son was still alive.

I was expected back to work in November 1990. My job was extremely sympathetic to my situation, but I could not manage to go back to work. Another lesson I learned from this is that all of us have our own journey of growing through grief. I did not allow the pressures of finances or work to force me into doing something that I knew I wasn't prepared to do. For every grieving parent reading this, learn to be truthful with your own journey. If you are not ready to leave the house, or walk the dog, say so. Never feel like you have to "get over it" and move on because that isn't realistic. Often, we set ourselves up for failure because we don't allow our heart the proper time to heal. I do not even know if my heart has fully healed as I write this, but I do know— I needed more time.

And you don't need to be afraid to say that. Time is, sometimes, the only way you will be able to cope with your pain. Overcompensating will suppress it. Avoiding it will not make it go away. So, I sat in my house and dealt with my hurt. Some days, I would fold his clothes and rearrange the toys. Other days, it was too hard for me to do anything. You have permission to have an "on day" and an "off day." Nobody knows the memory of your loved one. Use the time to heal!

Thankfully, the Vice President allowed me to extend my time off until January 1991. But when I arrived back to work in a new position, I found it extremely challenging. Granted, I was happy to still have a job, but I had to trust someone to care for my baby while I was at work. Those first few weeks, I kept looking at the phone worrying who was on the other line. I sighed in relief every time a caller was not calling about my girls. I still cried every day at work, and the anxiety of potential loss haunted me like the wicked witch of the west.

One day in particular I remember my manager asking if I could get a card from the group to express our condolences for a co-worker who had just lost a family member; I said no. He was surprised by my response, but I knew what I could handle. And I couldn't handle that. After talking to him about it, he suggested I seek a counselor and immediately I got angry and asked, "What is a counselor going to do for me?"

But a few weeks later, I went.

CHAPTER EIGHT

The Psychologist...

Psychologists have it hard. Most people do not go to therapists because life is swell. Most of us go because things are falling apart. Some of us are hesitant to open up and others of us can talk all day. As for me, I didn't even know why I was going, but I knew I had to go. My visits were interesting. We spent hours and hours talking about my son. The first session I went to, I didn't waste any time getting to the point. I was already reluctant and skeptical, so I asked a direct question to her: "What are you going to do for me? I want my son back!"

She just stared at me with the typical therapist gaze. I could tell she cared, but I knew her job was not to become too invested. She wanted me to get to the heart of my own sorrow, and I did. I think I did. I'm not sure if I did. The first couple of sessions, I cried the entire time. I couldn't talk much, and I was filled with sadness. You see, this was my first time ever dealing with death in my immediate family. For over 30 years, no one had ever died in my family. My parents were still alive. My cousins and friends were alive. So, I had no context of death at all, until Myles passed away.

One would think a mom or dad would go before their 3-year-old baby, so not only did the shock of loss hit me, but the fact that he was an innocent baby overwhelmed me. I was angry that nobody could bring him back. I was sad because I wanted him in my arms. All I could say for the first few sessions was "I want my son back."

The psychologist let me vent off my frustration day after day. She stared at me with that pensive, concentrated gaze. But one day, she finally whispered emphatically, "He is not coming back." It was like cold ice water being thrown in my face. I hated the sound of that truth, and I strongly disliked her for saying it. But it was the medicine I needed to begin my healing process.

It was apparent I was in the first stage of grieving; denial. Life made no sense. I didn't want to accept it. Denial is the stage where you still live as if you can change the past. You speak about your loved ones in the present tense because you have not yet reconciled that they are not going to come back.

The second stage of grief stayed with me for a long time. That stage is called ANGER. Let me tell you: if anger needed a photo next to its definition in a dictionary, it could've used my face. I have never been as angry as I was during those first few months. I was angry with the world because life was happening all around me as if nobody else cared that Myles had died. I remember driving down the street and seeing people chatting away. I would drive near schools and see children running into their classrooms. My entire body would become enflamed. The world kept moving. People kept laughing. School buses kept coming for children. Meanwhile, I would be there with my hands up screaming "Are you kidding? Myles just died." What is there to laugh about? What is there to celebrate? I was in a deep state of anger, but the world didn't stop; and I don't really know why I expected it to.

The 3rd stage was bargaining. Bargaining is when you say to God, "I will do anything if you bring my loved one back." You want what you want so bad that you make outlandish sacrifices to get what you want. God and I had an interesting relationship at that time. First of all, I was angry at Him too! I did not say anything to God. But what's interesting is that I didn't really start believing in Him until Myles died.

I grew up in a house where God was not mentioned. We did not have a Bible on the living room table. We did not go to church. We were "Easter" visitors, and we would go with a friend from time to time. But we weren't religious. I didn't pray or read Scripture. That wasn't how we did things in my home. But once my son died, I began to hear talk about how good God was. Once my son died, everyone had their opinion about this God, and how God had a better plan.

It made me furious!

It wasn't until a session with the psychologist that I realized: I was angry at a God whom I didn't even believe in. My anger with God began with the priest, and then it blossomed into hatred when my friends and family would say things like "God needed him," or "God had a plan," or "Myles is in a better place." I didn't want to hear that. So, I began to despise God because He robbed me of my son; that is, until my therapist asked me one day: "Did it ever occur to you that you didn't even pray to God before Myles died, and now you're angry at a God you didn't really believe in?" I had never thought of it that way, but it was true.

My introduction to God was camouflaged in sadness. I think if people had allowed me to learn who God was for myself, instead of telling me what God's will was for Myles, I would've been able to cope with it better. But the moment they put their two cents in and then blamed it on God, I was angry at both Him and them!

CHAPTER NINE

Dealing with Depression...

That's the thing about depression: A human being can survive almost anything, as long as she sees the end in sight. But depression is so insidious, and it compounds daily, that it's impossible to ever see the end. The fog is like a cage without a key.
-Elizabeth Wurtzel

That's what it felt like...a cage without a key. I felt trapped and helpless, you know, like those fairy tales where the princess can't get out of the castle. I stayed up many nights waiting for my "knight in shining armor" to come and rescue me from this horrible prison, but the more I waited, the more depressed I became.

There was no hope in sight. My only wish was that I could wake up from this dream and move on. But that wasn't happening. Every day seemed to drag on like a boring movie. I would go to work to get out of the house. But when I got to work, I just wanted to be home. I would get home and take care of my girls. But then I would stare at the television, or maybe the television was staring at me. I couldn't clean enough. I couldn't cook enough. I had nowhere to go. Parties didn't fascinate me anymore. Vacations didn't move me. I was depressed. I didn't know I was depressed, but every sign pointed to this cage without a key.

It set in deeper than I could imagine. This was the fourth stage of grief that still knocks on my door sometimes. Although I have two other beautiful children, a loving family and friends, I was always so sad. The best way I can describe it is that even when you want to smile, your mind tells you "Don't!" Boy, I thought anger lasted a long time, but depression seemed to last a lifetime. When people are depressed, they withdraw from everything. They attend your event, but they are not present. Spouses become confused and take it personal, but if you pay attention to the depressed person, they have withdrawn from everything--their job, their friends, their social clubs, and all. They are trying to find a place to hide, because the light of reality is too difficult to handle. Most of us who are depressed will try to overcompensate by pretending it doesn't matter, or we will escape from everything we know. We may eat ourselves into depression, or we may sleep ourselves into depression. Some of us make extreme changes in our appearance. Others of us lose ourselves and gain tremendous amounts of weight. We stop caring about the details. We are at a chilling standstill in life. The wind is blowing but we can't feel it. The sun is shining but we don't see it.

The best thing to do with friends who are depressed is to be present for them. Help them along by respecting their need for space. Don't make them feel bad for their current state. Just walk side-by-side with them and let them know you are there. Depressed or not, everybody wants to know that they are not alone.

So, I went through that---feeling alone at times, but the truth is, I had many branches of support around me. When it came time to go through the fifth stage, acceptance, I decided to write this book. I wasn't any less sad, but one day, I accepted the reality that it was permanent. Myles was not coming back and I had to learn to live without him. I had to focus on my girls, and make sure to give them a life worth living. Acceptance began the moment I realized, "Life will never be as it was before." As some would say, I made for myself a new normal.

My doctor prescribed anti-depressants to help me cope.

At first I refused to take them but I could not stop crying. I remember one weekend when my ex-husband picked the children up, I literally could not get out of bed. I felt that I was pinned down by a ton of bricks. I could not move so I slept in my jacket and my clothes. That episode taught me that every day is different. Some days are better than others, but never think you won't have "those" days. Everybody has them, and that's okay.

CHAPTER TEN

To the Church we go!

Church is a funny place to be! Depending on your culture, you can walk in and see a lot of different things. Some churches are so boring that you want to fall asleep. But there are other churches that make you feel like you're in a rock concert. The organ is pumping, the choir is singing. The mothers are shouting, and the teenagers are swinging on chandeliers. The preaching excites the listener, and the congregation becomes a big family. The church is a wonderful place for people who are used to it. But it can also be a scary place for folks like me!

My second Psychologist gave me my first Bible and suggested I go to church. *Oh no! It would've been better if she had said "go to the dentist."* I asked her why, and she said I needed to desensitize myself. It took me some time, but I began to attend church. The first time I stepped into a church after the funeral, I began to hyperventilate. Just imagine a regular looking woman walking in to the church doors. The hefty greeter smiles and says, "Right this way," and I start panting like I'm having an asthma attack. I wonder what that poor usher was thinking. It makes me laugh thinking about it now because she was looking at me as if I needed an Epi Pen. She had no clue what was happening to me, but I knew! I was having an anxiety attack right there in the church lobby.

I could not breathe, and I had to leave. It was the quickest church visit I've ever had. But the next time, I took my time and breathed a few times before entering. I sat in the very last row of the church. I looked around and felt...well, churchy. But it wasn't too bad.

I will tell you this---I was afraid of everything: the Pastor, the prayer, the choir, the people, the invitation to discipleship and the doxology. It felt like during the altar call, all eyes would shift to me. It felt like everyone knew what I didn't want them to know—that Myles had died, and I wasn't going to get him back. I felt judged even though no one was saying anything to me. I thought they would judge me if I was crying too much, and I did cry a lot. The songs made me cry, the prayer made me cry. The sermon made me cry! The offering envelopes made me cry! I was just a big cry baby, and that poor usher couldn't hand me enough tissue throughout the service. I think she bought a box just for me when she saw me coming.

The invitation to discipleship is the part of service when the Pastor extends an invitation to those who want to give their life to God. This part of the service made me so emotional because I felt an interesting pull. At times, I wanted to walk up and receive prayer. Other times, I was so scared and afraid of God that I would try to hide in my seat.

After many, many visits to church, I slowly began to cry less and feel a little better. I was not a member of the church, but I spoke with several ministers and even made contact with the Pastor. I was pleasantly surprised when the pastor called me back. He was such a nice man, and I was searching for answers. I wanted to know why my son had died. I wanted to know how God could be 'good all the time' and allow my son to die? Did this happen to him or me? Was I being punished for something we did or did not do? How could this happen? I needed to know!

I was given books on coping when losing a loved one. One book in particular was *When Bad Things Happen to Good People.* I read it until I reached a section that spoke about "The Book of Job." Job had lost everything, even his children. But the author didn't say "This was God's plan." The author didn't tie it all up with a beautiful red ribbon. Instead, he asked, "What kind of God would kill innocent children and visit unbearable anguish on the most devoted follower in order to win a bet with Satan?" I stopped reading at this point. For the first time, I felt relieved. I felt understood. Finally, someone was speaking my language and finally someone knew what I was going through. It felt so good to read on paper what I had been feeling in private!

CHAPTER ELEVEN

I'm not doing THAT because I'm dealing with THIS...

According to studies by the parental grief support group, "The Compassionate Friends" the nation's largest bereavement organization, 16% of all couples that experience the death of a child get divorced. It isn't uncommon for divorce to happen after death because a part of you dies when you bury a child.

Loss was one thing. But losing a child was an entirely different situation. It brought about a new kind of pain. You can't eat dinner without feeling it. You can't drive in the car without feeling it. Not one conversation goes by without thinking of it. It's a palpable, agonizing pain that comes to tear apart broken hearts; and if you do not seek healthy ways to heal, you'll end up harming everything around you.

We all know that every marriage has its problems...even small ones. Every marriage requires work, and when I got married, I was prepared to work. In fact, I expected to be married forever. I was the little girl with the fairy tale dream. I expected my husband and I to grow old together. But then, things suddenly changed. Every part of my reality shifted. I no longer wanted or could deal with disagreement. I no longer tolerated arguments. Life was just too black and white to focus on the gray areas. So on October 31, 1992 I decided to separate from my husband. I determined that if I had to deal with the loss of my son, I was not going to deal with anything else.

I remember it like it was yesterday. My sister and brother-in-law had just bought a house and moved back into the neighborhood on October 15, 1992. I asked my sister if my daughters and I could move in with her and her family; she said yes. I advised my husband that we would be moving out of the house and into my sister's house. I don't know if he believed me or not, but we kept living life as usual.

When that day arrived, he asked, "Are you still moving?" I looked at him with numbness in my eyes and said, "Yes." That was the beginning of the breakup.

I took the children to school and began moving. I packed our clothes, their toys, and their schoolbooks. The three of us slept on a pull-out couch every night. At times my daughters would ask, "When are we are going back home?" but I told them every time that we were not.

In February of the next year, my husband gave me a security deposit to move into a two-bedroom apartment. I walked into that place with the children's furniture and a couch. Eventually, I bought a bed and a kitchen table, but stuff didn't move me. When I moved out of my home, I didn't care about "things." I didn't care about much of anything. I just wanted my sanity. I just wanted my heart to stop hurting. I could care less about being a wife - I'm not doing THAT because I'm dealing with THIS... co-owner of a house, I just wanted 'OUT.' When the house was finally sold, we divided the profit and moved on.

Years later, I realized how little attention I gave to my husband. I did not console him very much during our tragedy. I didn't realize how much I had neglected his needs. I guess I was just so sad, so depressed and so unhappy—I couldn't see anything or anyone else. I was in a bubble and only focused on caring for my daughters. I don't remember having conversations about how he was feeling. I don't remember us going to counseling or trying to discuss ways to grieve together. When he tried to tell me stories about the good times we had with Myles, I cried. When he tried to lighten the moment, I cried. In his heart, he wanted to remember the good times but I wasn't ready to go there. I couldn't deal with that if I had to deal with this. It was too painful and I needed peace. I needed calm. I needed my son.

Just the mention of his name made me cry. The sight of his pictures, clothing, and toys made me cry. I cried so much, I think Lugene wanted to protect me from discussions about Myles. And it worked for a little while...but not long after, things went in the opposite direction. Lugene and I separated in October, 1992 and later we divorced.

CHAPTER TWELVE

My daughters...

For a long time, I felt guilty for depriving my daughters of a better life. I felt they had been stripped of my undivided attention. Even though I was (and am) a dedicated mother who loves her children, my sadness and depression interrupted my ability to parent them. I felt because I was so sad, I didn't or couldn't give as much love as I know I wanted to express. I felt bad for them, my youngest being three months old and the oldest being 7 years old when Myles died. As they grew older, I always felt I needed to do more to fill the gap.

Courtney, my youngest girl, said she had always known she had a brother from the pictures and stories, but it never really hit her until she was about 8 or 9. She remembers looking at her green photo album with pictures of Myles and began to sob. She contemplated talking with me about it but left it alone because it was a sensitive topic.

That is, until one day after Sunday dinner. She came downstairs crying hysterically. At first, she couldn't speak. After catching her breath, she blurted out, "I miss Myles."

That was the day she fully understood what had happened to him. Later, she confessed to me that she thought it was her fault. She thought that if she had never been born, Myles would still be here. Somehow, she put together that she was the reason her brother and sister were in camp in the first place. If she hadn't been the baby I was tending to, they would've been home with me. This was not true because every summer, Myles and Quiana would go to summer camp. But still, I allowed Courtney to vent her feelings to me.

My stepdaughter, Tamika, Lugene's daughter from a previous relationship, also had an interesting experience with loss. At the time of Myles' death, she was 15 years old. She made me realize that every child processes death differently, and most children—no matter how young or old—blame it on themselves. Tamika confessed to having nightmares every night about Myles. She couldn't sleep in her own room for months. She didn't even talk about Myles because she didn't want to burden her mom or Lugene, and she carried this around for a very long time. My oldest daughter, Quiana, is a creative soul who has photogenic memory. She can recall details about that time in our lives that I don't remember. Her process was different than the others. She used her pain to fuel her passions. She became a very outgoing and bright ray of sunshine. She is talkative, optimistic, and full of energy. She and Courtney both are risk-takers. They aren't afraid to fail. They have so much life and heart, and they loved their brother very much.

Children are the heartbeat and soul of their parents. When your child confesses his or her pain to you, empathize with them.

Hug them. Love them. Assure them. Correcting their feelings won't make the situation go away. Courtney took on the blame for Myles' death. Courtney said she felt the need to get Lugene and I back together. Most children will find themselves responsible, when of course, the issues run much deeper. But the key is, I allowed my children to tell me their experience. They always knew that they could come to me and talk to me about anything. That is one of the greatest benefits to having two beautiful and respectfully pleasant girls. They are not just my children; they are my friends. We go out together. We vacation from time to time. We cry our eyes out together, and we laugh uncontrollably. The bond we have cannot be broken.

Thankfully, Courtney stopped feeling guilty about the past after she began her walk with Christ and was baptized. She felt a lot better about herself and also became very happy for me because I began to accept God into my life; it was the best thing for her. And another funny detail is that I felt guilty about their childhood, but they loved their experience! My girls remember having a vibrant and happy childhood. Granted, they knew that I was emotionally closed off, but they loved me through my pain. They told me years later that they were so happy with the way I raised them. I saw it differently, and their love reshaped me. It gave me hope. It secured me as their mom. I no longer walked around wishing I could re-do my past. I learned to take every day as an opportunity to grow, learn, and move forward. I know for sure that I am a better woman because of my girls. I love them more than life itself, and there's nothing they can do to change that.

CHAPTER THIRTEEN

I'm still standing but questioning...

L ife is not about the destination; it's about the journey. Conquering loss is not about the day you stop crying; it's about the day when your tears sing a new song. Each episode in this drama that we call life teaches us something about ourselves. It reveals what we treasure. It reveals who we really are. When I look back at my life, I can't believe I'm still here. I can't believe I survived the storm of losing my son. The heart break I experienced was unimaginable. I never thought I would stop crying. I never thought the anger would go away. I never thought I would accept it. But one day, I realized: I'm still standing.

And so are you. You are still standing despite the odds. You are still standing despite the tears. You are still standing even though you thought for sure that the pain you felt would drive you crazy. You are standing, and that is a miracle in itself. Give yourself some credit! Take yourself out to dinner. Go to a comedy show and laugh until you cry. Why? Because you deserve it. After all that your heart has survived, and after all the sleepless nights, your ability to keep it moving, taking it one step at a time, says "I'm standing." Think about what you've accomplished despite the pain. Think about the people you've helped because of your pain. Oftentimes, I wonder how life would've been different if Myles had not died. I think about if he would be married by now, or where he would be working? And I can't help but wonder these things. Still and all, I know that this experience made me a more caring person. I truly care about people in a deep way. It also made me a more cautious person. I have learned to take life seriously, and not to leave anything to "assumption." But it has also made me a more intentional person. Life is too short to mourn over things that don't matter. Suddenly, I lost tolerance for nonsense. If I didn't want to go, I didn't go. If I didn't want to stay, I didn't stay. One of the greatest things this experience taught me is how to be honest with myself. I lived my life trying to please so many people, and inwardly I was unhappy.

The truth is it is still difficult. Life is not an easy walk in the park. Some days are easier than others, but one thing I know for sure: there is no way I would have made it without God. There is no way I would have had the ability to raise two beautiful daughters with morals and values. There is no way I could've found the confidence to instill in them right and wrong. There's no way I would have had the strength to earn an Associate's degree, Bachelor's degree and Masters of Business Administration without God.

The Associate's degree was the most rewarding because it showed me that I could still accomplish something. The good news is you can accomplish something too! Tragedy is not the final scene. This just may be your intermission. Your life is not over. Your heart is still beating. If you still have a dream for your future, you can become whatever you put your mind to.

CHAPTER FOURTEEN

What are your dreams?

I was able to keep my job and that was a miracle. My mind still wonders about some things. I wish I knew for sure what my life's purpose was. I wish I had a clearer path and more confidence, but when I think about what I've conquered, I no longer make myself feel guilty about things I cannot change. I know there is more to my life than what I'm doing right now, but the fact that I am thinking about doing more says that my dream has not died. All of us have a dream for our lives. We want to help the world by living an intentional life. None of us, me included, want to work at a job that has no value. We don't want to live in a house that doesn't give us peace. What are your dreams? I don't have it all figured out, but I don't want you to think your life is over. I always dreamed of helping people to become more healthy and fit. I want to become a personal trainer and help people to see that with a little determination and discipline, you can do anything. I also dream of sitting out on the beach and enjoying life. I know I have a real passion for children--that's why losing Myles hurt so much--but now, instead of running away from it, I run toward it. I have conquered my fear of taking care of other people's children. Now, all my family knows to turn to me with the kids. I love kids! They are precious and perfect. And focusing on what you love is the key to conquering what you fear.

I know that every experience in my life was to help someone, because I love helping people. What about you? What do you love to do? What are your dreams? What is your purpose? Sometimes we can let the cloud of grief rain over every parade in our lives, but don't forget to find the sun in the midst of your sadness. There's always something to be thankful for. When I didn't know what else to be thankful for, I would walk into my girls' bedroom, and just smile. They were enough to remind me-my life matters.

And the same is true for every hurting heart reading this book. Your life really matters. You are an amazing person. You have endured one of the most difficult tragedies in life, but still, you are standing! With all my blessings, I still question why Myles is not here. I still ask myself why God allowed him to die. It's twenty-one years later and some days are still very difficult. Some chapters were harder to write than others. All of us, including me, are a work-in-progress. Nothing in life is as easy as it seems. Everything comes with ups and downs. But the day you stop blaming yourself is the day you can truly make a change. I am happy to know that my experience can help someone else to cope with their pain. I don't have everything figured out, but when you think about it...nobody does! The treasure of life is when we can take the gems of our past and use them to help others discover their future.

CHAPTER FIFTEEN

The Church journey...

I continued going to the Baptist Church every Sunday. Of course, I would always sit in the last row looking around at the people, the ministers, and ushers. *Poor ushers.* They didn't know what to do with me. But come to think of it, I didn't know what to do with me. I was scared to death. I knew I needed this community to help me heal, but I didn't always want to be there. It was like I was wrestling with myself. Some mornings, I would talk myself out of going just because I didn't want to be stared at. Other Sundays I realized that all of this was in my mind, and I would go anyway and have a wonderful time.

Each time I went to church, I would try to follow the program, and I tried to understand the message. When the choir sang, I thought I would die. Every time they sang, I sobbed. The song could be "Oh Happy Day" but I knew by the end of the song, I was going to cry.

You know, music has a way of moving the soul. It causes you to reflect on hidden hurts and allows you the opportunity to heal over time. When your friends are going through loss or pain, buy them a CD that will give them permission to heal. If they enjoy jazz, purchase something that they can listen to near the gravesite. I personally found it to be very soothing to sit next to Myles' tombstone. When he first died, I probably went there once a month. Especially on his birthday (March 10th), Mother's Day, Christmas, and on the anniversary of his death, I had to be there. This was my pattern for years and although my brother, Jr., was concerned about my frequent visits to the gravesite, he realized I needed this time to reflect with my son. I didn't always cry, though. Sometimes I just sat there in silence. Sometimes I talked to him as if he were sitting right there with me. If the weather was nice, I would bring a blanket and flowers. I enjoyed thinking about him. I imagined hugging him, and I always told him how much I missed him.

One time I brought his "bat mobile" and put it on his tomb stone and surprisingly it stayed there. But at some point, I decided to take it back home because I didn't want it to disappear. These were my rituals. This was one method to my madness. If you are grieving right now, I encourage you to find out what works for you. Whatever brings you real joy, repeat that activity until you can process your pain. Take your time. Cry as much as you need to.

Everyone has different ways to cope with loss. As friends and family members, your job is to support us through our pain. Forcing us to "get over it" is insensitive. Telling us your opinion, especially when we haven't asked you, is worse than saying nothing at all. What if it were your son? What if you got the call that something tragic had happened to someone you love very deeply? I've found out that it's very easy to give an opinion when it hasn't happened to you, it's much more difficult to go through it yourself.

The church I went to allowed me the time to grieve in my own way. I never felt rushed or belittled. The sermons always gave me hope. Very often, I felt as if the pastor was talking directly to me. Eventually, I started to sit a little closer, not quite in the last row but still in the back of the church. I would still look around afraid to talk to people, but this time, I would smile if my eye caught someone else's eye. One particular Sunday, a different Minister had to preach, or I should say read their sermon. I had no idea what the minister was trying to convey. I was confused all over again. Ministers and preachers, it really matters what you say. You never know who is listening to you on Sunday and you really need to take into consideration how your words will help or hurt someone.

I needed that experience because it taught me something about myself. I enjoyed the Pastor's style, but I had to learn how to focus on the message and not the messenger. The key, for me, was to listen to the heart of the sermon, and ask God for understanding because there might come a day when the pastor would not be there. When I took my mind off the person speaking and started to focus on the message itself, that is when I started—little by little—to take baby steps toward establishing a relationship with God. In 2007, I joined the Church, and I was excited about doing so. I wanted to learn more about Christians, and I wanted to feel better. But ultimately, I wanted to get closer to God.

CHAPTER SIXTEEN

What I know...

What I know is that Myles brought me so much joy. The joy experienced between a mother and her son is unlike any other. What I also know is that sharing my heart with family and friends is what began my process of healing. Talking with ministers, doctors and people who experienced the same loss is priceless. It's a weight lifted off one's shoulders when you can speak with someone who has lost a child. It gives you a feeling that 'finally someone understands exactly what I'm feeling,' and you don't feel so alone.

What I know is that talking about your story always helps your heart to heal. When you share these feelings with others, and when others share their pain with you, empathy is born for that person. You have been there, and you will want to listen to their story because by listening you will help them to get things off their chest. So don't be shy. Talk it out. Listen with your heart. And bring your entire self to the table.

What I also know is that I can't improve myself if I'm still depressed. When I was asked to do something that I didn't want to do, I had to choose between "saying yes" or bringing negative energy into the room. I chose to say "no" until I was ready because depression is negative energy. It's a heavy weight that clouds your judgment and ruins your joy. If you're not ready, don't commit to it. Just say no. But if you know that it's time to make some new steps, give life a try. Don't let depression run your life. If you do, you will wake up years later in the same place you were in when you first got the call that your loved one had died.

Pet Peeves...

Sometimes people say the wrong thing and it can cause grieving mothers or fathers to become very angry. I get it. People want to say something but they don't know what to say. For that reason, I designed a little "pet peeves" list. I'm hoping you will consider these recommendations as helpful tips when you encounter someone who has lost a child or a loved one.

1. *You have your daughters.*

When someone would say to me "I know you lost your son, but you have your daughters," I would become so very angry. Certainly, I love my daughters, but the love I have for them has nothing to do with Myles. One child or fifteen children will never replace the one you lost. It doesn't work that way. There is a special place in a mother's heart for all of her children. When her child dies, a part of her dies, too.

2. *It was God's plan.*

When someone would say "It was God's plan," I would immediately respond, "Well that's a stupid plan. What kind of God would plan to take away my child? It's stupid." Other members of my family are okay with this statement, but not me. In my opinion, before you blame God, be sure that God actually feels that way about it. Most of us just say what we have heard others say, and it can do more harm than good.

3. *Talk to God.*

With time, all things heal. But when people said, "Just pray and talk to God," it would confuse me. How could they expect me to talk to the person who took my son away? I had nothing to say to God; at least nothing good to say—so talking to Him wouldn't have worked for me. What would've been better is if someone had taught me how to pray. I may have been more open if they took my questions into consideration and didn't force me to make amends with my pain on their terms. When hearts are bleeding, be sensitive to their pain.

Walk them through prayer, don't just impose it on them.

4. **"Myles was an angel that God wanted, or He's in a better place."**

I understand that church jargon helps some people, but it didn't help me. Everybody is different. Some don't believe what you believe. Some don't accept the cookie-cutter "angel" response as justification for loss. In my mind, the best place for Myles was in my arms, or in his home with his family. This statement was said without much thought, and I took it personally. You may mean no harm, but be mindful of other people's journey. If they are not there yet, don't force faith down anyone's throat. Just help them by being present with them.

5. *"God gives and He can take away."*

This statement left me with more questions than answers. It didn't resolve the tension in my heart. After someone said it, I didn't have an epiphany. I was oftentimes more confused and ticked off. Why would God give a gift only to take it away? If God didn't want me to have it, why would He give it to me in the first place? What I learned through this experience is that presence matters more than words. A hug is probably enough. Let the person grieving talk. Nod. Hug them. Be there for them. I didn't even know God at the time, and people were shoving all of this "God-talk" down my throat.

Relax...please!

6. *Read the Bible.*

I had never owned a Bible, and when someone gifted it to me, I didn't know what to do with it. Here again we have someone assuming about faith that wasn't true for me. I didn't have a relationship with God. It would've been better if they had read it with me. Maybe I would've had more peace if someone had given me a practical guide on how to understand the Bible. But I was just told, "Read it,"

without anything else said. The lesson here is simple. If you want to help me, guide me. Don't just inform me!

7. *Go to a support group.*

Initially, I thought this was useless. Here's a group of strangers who know nothing about me or Myles...why would I go there and spill out my heart to them? Now that I look back on it, I can see how this could've helped. But I wasn't ready yet. Learn to allow everyone to have their own developmental process of healing. Therapy was emotional, and it didn't always yield the results that others expected it to yield. I am grateful for the time I spent there, but she never helped me to bring Myles back. The lesson here is simple: stop assuming that everyone will cope with loss the same way you do. For some, it may be therapy. For others, it may be a support group. For another it could be finding a church. But everyone's situation is different. Give options!

8. *People wanted to buy me things to make me feel better.*

I was always an independent person. I worked for everything I own, and I didn't like feeling like the "pity" person. When people wanted to do things for me, my guard went up. It reminded me that I wasn't well. It was overkill at first. People, in their attempt to help me, made me paranoid. I was fine. I could do certain things on my own. The key is, ask me. Don't assume I am helpless. If I need your help, I will let you know. It's much easier to respect the space of the grieving heart, than to crowd them and make them feel handicap. The pain was already unbearable. By people "doing" for me (without my permission), it made it even more obvious that Myles was not around.

Why I wrote this book...

This book will probably not be like most. I wanted to write from the heart of a mom who is still hurting but learning to dance with a limp. This book is not an admission that 'God is good all the time' and He knows what He's doing. It's a personal memoir written by someone who didn't know God, did not have a Bible growing up...but does now. It's about someone who went to church only on Easter Sunday and continued that pattern even while married and never tried to know Him. It's a story about living while suffering the heartbreak of losing a child and being angry with God because people told me it was God's plan. But here's the good news— I'm still standing, and I can tell my story to help others. I hope this book has helped you to know that you are not alone. Even though the pain and suffering are so relentless and you think you will not survive, I'm writing to tell you, you will.

When you feel down, and when you don't know what to do, use your grief for the good. Find an opportunity to help someone else. Find a friend that you can talk to. Write your thoughts in a journal. Search for a support group, and don't be afraid to tell the truth. If you love children, volunteer at a children's hospital. If you like to read, hang out at the library and read a story to senior citizens. There is so much more to life than the saddest day of your journey. Remember that your life still matters. God was with me even when I was angry at him, and I'm sure God is still with me now. Am I saying, "God is good all the time?" Not really. If I am honest, I'm still questioning what that means. But what I do know is that God will help you. You may be at a low point today, but tomorrow is another day. You may not want to live anymore, but you're still here! Who knows what lies in your future? If you give up now, you may miss the rainbow at the end of the storm.

I'm Still Here (Poem)...

Please don't mourn for me.

I'm still here, though you don't see.

I'm right by your side each night and day and within your heart I long to stay.

My body is gone but I'm always near. I'm everything you feel, see or hear.

My spirit is free, but I'll never depart as long as you keep me alive in your heart.

I'll never wander out of your sight–

I'm the brightest star on a summer night.

I'll never be beyond your reach–

I'm the warm moist sand when you're at the beach.

I'm the colorful leaves when fall comes around and the pure white snow that blankets the ground.

I'm the beautiful flowers of which you're so fond, The clear cool water in a quiet pond.

I'm the first bright blossom you'll see in the spring, The first warm raindrop that April will bring.

I'm the first ray of light when the sun starts to shine, and you'll see that the face in the moon is mine.

When you start thinking there's no one to love you, you can talk to me through the Lord above you.

I'll whisper my answer through the leaves on the trees, and you'll feel my presence in the soft summer breeze.

I'm the hot salty tears that flow when you weep

and the beautiful dreams that come while you sleep.

I'm the smile you see on a baby's face.

Just look for me, friend, I'm everyplace!

-Author Unknown

DEDICATION

This book is dedicated to my sunshine, Myles.

Dear Mommy,

You spent years drowning in thoughts of worry, fear, and sadness. We're here to tell you after twenty-three years... it's time for you to live in peace. Peace with yourself as an outstanding woman, mother and best friend. You are our greatest blessing. In cloudy moments, when you thought you weren't enough, you were wrong. You blessed us with unconditional love, an ocean of kisses, and a field of hugs. You rubbed every bump, cured every sickness, laughed at every joke, and always stood right by our side. Our childhood was filled with joy and that is because of you. Our days are spent dreaming of our future, and when we think of it, we realize that we want to be just like you.

I pray the love you feel from us will shower you with peace. You are beautiful from the inside out and it's time you understand that you, my darling, are enough!

Love,
Courtney and Quiana

Acknowledgments...

There are many people who had a part in helping with this book.

First and foremost, to the loves of my life. Quiana and Courtney, I want to thank you for being so supportive throughout the entire process. You were with me while writing this book and you relived the details even when they were too painful to communicate. The two of you are my rock—a mother's dream come true. Thank you so much for your encouragement. I Love You more than you could ever know!

My dear family - my parents, brothers and sister who walked with me day after day while enduring their own sense of loss with Myles' death. To my sister, Simone, thank you so very much for allowing me to be the person I've become and for accepting me. Thank you for staying by my side and for always being willing to help me, Quiana and Courtney.

My dear close extended family and friends who always listened when I needed to release frustration and tears. Thank you for still loving me. Special thanks to my close girlfriends and cousins who continue to travel with me and help me to enjoy life. If I tried to name each of you, this acknowledgments page would never end! But thank you so much! Each of you has a special place in my heart!

Thank you to my brother-in-law Tyrone for always being willing to help. Tyrone, you helped me to write this book by providing crucial details, even when I couldn't remember. Thank you!

Thank you to my ex-husband Lugene. We suffered the same loss. We cried the same tears. Thank you for reminding me of the joy Myles brought me. Thank you for your invaluable contributions and support, which enabled me to write this book.

CONTACT AUTHOR

Phyllis Owens
Email: Mylesoflife@gmail.com